Cash Flow

Seven Steps to Successful

Real Estate Investing

by

Douglas Crowley

Dedication

To Sandy: my partner and best friend in real estate, in marriage and in life. Thanks for all your help.

Cash Flow

Seven Steps to Successful Real Estate Investing

by Douglas Crowley

www.cashflow7stepstosuccessfulrealestateinvesting.com

© 2013 Douglas Crowley. ALL RIGHTS RESERVED

PUBLISHED BY 10-10-10 PUBLISHING

ISBN: 978-1-927677-76-6

7 Steps to Cash Flow

Contents

Foreword... 4

Cash Flow is Good.. 7

Plan to Succeed - Succeed with a Plan...............19

Light the Road to Success - Learn Your Market.............27

Systems Lead to Success...39

Rev Up the Horse Power in Your Power Team...............51

Show Me the Money...67

Marketing - The Key to Success...........................79

The Joy of Tenants...86

Go Build Your Wealth..101

Foreword

Cash Flow by Douglas Crowley can help you attain success in real estate investing by understanding that cash flow is king. Within these pages, you learn how to calculate your deals to insure you achieve positive cash flow. You will avoid costly mistakes and speed your path in real estate investing. Plus, Douglas Crowley loaded *Cash Flow's* chapters with web links so you stay current with the latest real estate markets and concepts as your investments evolve.

Cash Flow guides you step by step through each process. You are assured of success. You learn how to set up your business plan and how to quickly analyze your real estate market. Douglas Crowley's real life examples provide details instead of vague concepts in a straightforward manner from starting your real estate investing business to cashing your tenants' rent checks.

In this book:

- You learn the importance of systems in business.
- You learn the advantages of developing your power team to help you succeed.
- You learn how to raise money and how important marketing is to your success.
- You learn the ins and outs of being a landlord.
- You learn seven key ingredients to build your wealth in Real Estate.

Raymond Aaron

NY TIMES Best Selling Author

www.millionairebusinessbootcamp.com

Chapter 1

Cash Flow is Good

Welcome to real estate investing. There are many ways to make or lose money in real estate. The purpose of this book is to maximize your ability to make money while reducing your chances of losing money. Thank you for acquiring this book and more importantly for opening the cover to see what's inside.

Through these pages, I'll take you on a journey of how I started investing in real estate. We'll cover developing your business model and setting up the successful formula that worked for me. I'll spend a little time talking about the importance of the development of your power team; how to get funding; the importance of marketing and branding; as well as the challenges of property management. All in all, I'll lead you step-by-step through my first three properties as an investor.

First, let's take a moment and talk about WHY? WHY invest in real estate? Any endeavor in life that we embark upon has to have a reason. If we cannot answer WHY we are doing something, we are unlikely to complete the goal. Why did you acquire and start reading this book? I hope you wish to learn how to improve your cash flow and thus the quality of your life.

As we start this journey through the seven successful steps to real estate investing, I feel I need to tell a little bit of my story to bring credibility to the process; to explain why I took this route to diversify my assets and hopefully increase my wealth enough to pass something on to my family.

7 Steps to Cash Flow

I retired from government service in June of 2012 having worked over 27 years as a meteorologist. During that time, I had managed to save enough money to live a modestly comfortable lifestyle. But, the previous 12 years of the country's bad economy had destroyed more than a third of my savings. I experienced almost daily concerns about the ability of my savings to last the rest of our lives.

I am very lucky as a retired federal employee to have a small defined benefit plan. But, I am under the new retirement plan so I must count on savings and Social Security to supplement my retirement needs. At the time I retired, I could have purchased a single pay lifetime annuity for myself and my wife that would have paid out less than $400 a month for every hundred thousand dollars invested. These annuities are designed so that by the time we die, any money left in the pot goes to the insurance company selling the annuity. Does that seem fair to you? I didn't think so either! Would you rather any monies left go to your family, were that possible? And after seeing two major market crashes in the past dozen years and near zero return on my savings, I felt the need to find a solution that did not involve the stock market, CDs, savings, or annuities.

It turns out that saving for retirement was easier than developing a plan to draw down the money over the remainder of our lives. There are simply too many unknowns. How long will my wife and I live? Will it support our lifestyle? How much will inflation grow? How high will taxes rise? Will our health hold up? Will Social Security provide the supplement I had been promised during my fifty years of work?

I spent the last three years as an employee trying to figure out how to spread my savings and other benefits to carry myself and my wife through our expected lifetimes and then some. There wasn't a month that went by that I did not spend fifteen or twenty minutes with my wife discussing withdrawal options in many derivations to ensure our money could last through both our lifetimes. Most of the answers required living a more austere lifestyle. I needed to find another solution besides the stock market and my government controlled benefits. The one recurring option was real estate.

I had been a real estate agent in my youth and my dad was a real estate broker in his later years. With the crash in the housing market and the historically low interest rates, real estate investing seemed to offer a solution. Could it be the right solution?

In August 2010, we went to a Rich Dad Education introductory program for building wealth through real estate investing. A very motivated and bright young man by the name of Marc Hrisko introduced us to Rich Dad's advanced training program. Marc became very successful using real estate; in fact he has a book out titled *Kangaroo Millionaire*. While I would not mind becoming a millionaire, my hope was simply to provide additional income security and possibly build some wealth to pass along.

Real Estate seemed the most logical answer.

I realized that the federal government controlled my defined-benefit annuity, my thrift savings plan (federal equivalent of private 401K matching), and any Social Security supplement I was to receive. I was in almost the same shape as an Enron or Lehman Brother's employee. All my resources were in one basket and controlled by one entity, the U.S. Government. While I don't expect the government to close up shop, it can and likely will reduce my benefits and tax me more in the process. So, just like the leaders of those failed companies, our government is telling us it will all work out. Yet, it remains dysfunctional and supportive of everything that caused the second greatest depression in American history.

That's my big WHY. **SELF-PRESERVATION.** I had to figure out another way to bring in additional money to support even a modest lifestyle in retirement. To compound matters, I was diagnosed with macular degeneration in 2007. The disease's progression finally impacted my ability to keep up with the tasks and training required in my career as a meteorologist. Since my vision limitation would impact options to find other gainful employment or engage in volunteer activities I was looking forward to pursuing, the logical conclusion was to create my own business opportunity.

You may decide to follow my steps into Real Estate for cash flow or open your own business. Whatever you decide, you must have a great WHY. And just making money will not cut it. The right WHY will allow you to translate desire and knowledge into action! You must take action to be successful. It does not matter if you are retired, at the peak of your career or just getting started. You should consider the end game and decide if you intend to provide for yourself or hope that someone else will provide for you. If you intend to take care of yourself, you must consider doing more than working and saving in traditional IRAs.

Before we were introduced to Rich Dad Education by

Marc Hrisko, I had already read *Rich Dad Poor Dad*, by Robert Kiyosaki. I came away with three overriding themes. First is the failure of our public school systems to provide basic financial literacy. The second theme was that people get rich by buying assets and not things. The third is that once individuals have acquired money the best place to store their wealth is in property.

When I thought about the housing crisis and the fact that more than six million American families had lost their homes, I realized the need for safe, quality housing in good neighborhoods with good schools would rise. Just over two years ago, I was introduced to the availability of sound real estate education. It was not cheap, but on the other hand I felt it was much less expensive than just one bad investment. So, my wife and I enrolled in a few classes. This turned out to be a wise investment for us. Not only have the classes provided great training, the presentation structure has also provided tremendous networking opportunities. But taking classes is not the only way to educate yourself. You can accomplish it with books and/or find local mentors to help you along.

I was exposed to the housing decline during the recession in the early 1980s and again with the most recent crisis. Hundreds of real estate gurus told us over the past decade that we, too, could be instant millionaires in the real estate market. Some made millions. Many lost. Many more signed up to take courses, read books and then did nothing. So, if you're one of the many that are comfortable sitting on the sidelines rather than getting involved in the game, now might be a good time to close this book and move on with your life as it is today.

Good, I'm glad you stayed with me.

I decided on real estate investing because it offered the most options, the best returns, favorable tax laws and a great opportunity to help a few of the many millions of families that have been displaced from their homes. I realized early on that I could buy a $100,000 house, rent it for $900 per month, receive tax depreciation, deduct business expenses before income earnings and end up with a gross return of $500 per month, but only have a tax liability at a reduced investment rate for about $300 per month in earnings. That meant that now I would bring home 25% more money per month than purchasing an annuity, have a lower tax rate, have an asset that the tenants pay for, and a house to leave to my heirs. Learning to buy right and how to leverage can accelerate your returns. This is Cash Flow we can all use!

Real Estate provides diversification that I sorely needed. Most likely, you do, too. People generally count their personal homes as a real estate investment. While it is a great asset that provides shelter for you and your family, it does not put money in your pockets. Therefore, it is an asset that's really a liability.

There are a few drawbacks to this pathway. You have to either manage the property or pay a property manager. The latter obviously reduces your earnings. However, in the end, you're still much better off than if you purchase today's subpar annuities. Can you lose money in real estate? Of course you can. Everything has risk. But with housing near forty year lows and interest rates at all-time historical lows, you have a pretty good chance of winning this game. Unlike stocks that may go to zero, think Enron, the only land I know of that goes to zero might include a Three Mile Island meltdown or Chernobyl incident, or possibly a flood zone where rebuilding isn't allowed. Fortunately, in these cases, either an energy company or a government steps in and provides some reimbursement. These risks can be mitigated with education and due diligence. Other hazards can be covered by insurance.

Throughout the following chapters, I will explore seven steps to successful real estate investing. The first step is to develop a business model. Second, you have to learn the market. Third, you need to set up a system or process toward success.

Fourth, this is an essential step; you must develop your power team. For the fifth step, we'll talk about finding money sources. In step six, we will discuss marketing. And finally, step seven will cover property management.

My mission for this book is to share with you the process and growth I went through as I acquired each of my first three rental properties. I want to help you get off the bleachers and into the game. I will serve as your coach to help you think a bit differently and to do things a little differently.

Everyone has an opportunity—it only takes commitment and action—to add an additional $1000 to your monthly income or $4000 or $8000 if that's how far you want to go. Real Estate Investing is also a great vehicle to become the millionaire within you if that's the direction you choose to go. The course you choose is up to you. You only have to take action. Remember, if you're running in place the scenery never changes. Get off the treadmill of life and take in a different view.

Chapter 2

Plan to Succeed - Succeed with a Plan

STEP ONE: Develop a Business Plan

Like the old saying goes: Fail to Plan and you Plan to Fail. Developing a business plan is a critical step to success. Less than 20% of new businesses in America today survive their first year and another half are gone by the second. A majority of those that failed did not have a business plan. A good business plan will define your mission; describe your business purpose; set up your business goals; structure your asset protection; and break down your finances for the first few years, which will include start up costs and earnings. You will not know many of these structures or costs ahead of time. Your goal is to make a best estimate or projection of what you think the business can do during its first week, first month, first year, and beyond.

Let's start by addressing your mission statement. This is a short summary, usually a sentence or two, which states the purpose of your business. In my case it reads: "Provide safe, quality housing at the best value in my market." As you can see, that is simple and straightforward. If I provide the best value for a quality house in a safe environment, my business remains ahead of the competition. It also means I will have a better chance of renting to higher-quality tenants. My goal will always be that of acting as a good landlord who takes care of my tenants so both of us take care of the property.

You, too, might create a simple straightforward mission statement, but remember...this is not a hobby; it is a business.

The mission statement can also be explained as the "WHY" of your business. Naturally you want to make money. However, there has to be a stronger motivation if you want to become successful. A stronger motivation gets to the root of why you want to start this business in real estate investing or any other endeavor you select. The motivation for you must be stronger than simply to go out and do something to make money. In my case, the overwhelming WHY is to build wealth for my family and more importantly, to show through example that they, too, can become successful real estate investors.

The next thing you want to address is the purpose of your business. This will help you design the process or systems to match your mission and goals. The purpose may be redundant to the mission statement but goes into greater detail. Even more than that, it discusses the niche your business will fill. It describes why there is a need for your business. As I mentioned in Chapter 1, with over six million families suffering the loss of their homes, my purpose is to provide a safe, affordable home for them. These families have been living in homes of their own, often times for many years. It was devastating to give up those private sanctuaries. Especially if they were forced to give up the family pet, too, because the apartment they moved into had no green zone or a "no pet" policy. Abandoning four-legged companions compounds the stress of already difficult times. Your niche should be to fill a void not provided for these displaced families by the traditional property management companies.

Your business plan or model should also include goals. Goals should be specific and have a timeline associated with them. The difference in a dream and a goal is the timeline. For example, you might state: *I will buy and rent my first house within ninety days.* If you have another job or business, you may wish to be more flexible with your goals and timelines. In that case you might state: *I will buy one single family rental unit every two years until I have ten homes.*

Goals should cover other specifics as well. Let's consider one of my goals, *I want each rental to gross a minimum of $250 per month and provide a return on my investment of at least 15%.* My goal was originally $200 per door and at least a 12% return, but I realized I could do better so I increased the 12% to 15%. I have done much better than that. I'm averaging over $350 per door, and my return on investment is closer to 20%. It took my wife and me fifteen months to acquire our first three rentals. We purchased those homes below market value so the expectation of capital appreciation is high as well.

You can be flexible with your numbers if you have sound financial reasoning such as a great deal with tremendous capital appreciation. This may allow for a slightly lower cash-on-cash return on your investment. Be sure any adjustments to your stated numbers are based on intellect and not emotions. Also keep in mind, this book is about cash flow. If you buy the home right, have good cash flow and a decent return on your investment, you'll be able to weather any additional pullbacks the housing market may offer.

A very important part of your business plan will also include your business structure. You can set up as a sole proprietorship, an LLC or a corporation. While I'm not an asset protection attorney, most will tell you that a sole proprietorship has no setup fees but it can cost you dearly. The amount of asset protection you desire and type of LLC or corporation you set up may be predetermined by what resources or assets you possess. The greater those assets the more critical it is that you set up your business structure before you purchase your first rental unit. Buy and hold rentals in single-family units tend to work very well under an LLC as a pass-through entity on your personal taxes. If you opt for an LLC, your asset attorney can help you set that up and obtain a tax ID number. Be sure you get professional advice in this arena.

We will get into more detail about your power team in Step Four. Until then, just know that two very important members of your team will be your accountant and attorney. They will help you determine the best business structure to set up for asset protection and tax purposes.

Think of asset protection as additional insurance. The type of business entity you set up will help isolate liabilities to that business and not your personal assets. For this to succeed, you need to run your business like a business, keep personal and business money separate, and maintain all the proper paperwork and documents required for that entity.

Other features of the business plan will include your power team members, such as banking contacts, insurance provider, and vendors in your area. As stated earlier it will also include a projection of start-up costs, operating expenses, and expected earnings projected quarterly over the next three years. The business plan is not fixed in stone, it's a guideline that helps you plan your business objectives and provides credibility so potential investors feel you operate from a sound premise.

Two additional sources to help with the business plan are the internet and your local business incubator, the latter if you like more hands-on-support.

Chapter 3

Light the Road to Success - Learn Your Market

STEP TWO: Learn the Market Where You Want to

Invest

Let's take a moment and talk a little bit about the various

real estate investments. The most basic and common investment

is a single-family home. This path works great for the diversified

investor that has just one home or the professional real estate investor who may have hundreds. The next option is the duplex, tri-plex and the four-plex. These are consolidated in the single-family class when it comes to funding. Once you move to a five door unit and higher you enter the apartment world and commercial funding. These designations cover the basic properties in which people live. Next are the four major classes in commercial real estate. In addition to apartments, there are warehouse, retail and office spaces that can be invested in and rented for cash flow.

Single-family properties are typically the best starting level option. Whenever you buy property you must follow the first rule; buy it for the right price. The second biggest consideration you need to think about is your exit strategy, or how to resell the property. A single-family home is the easiest to resell. The duplex would be next but typically reduces the number of potential buyers by a considerable amount. However it can be the perfect option for a young person or couple to get their first starter home and rent out the other side to help cover the mortgage. Once you move into three units or more you will find their appreciation rate may no longer match that of the single-family market. These multi-unit dwellings will typically be valued on their income potential. This is referred to as the CAP (capitalization rate).

Let me take a moment to explain CAP rate. CAP rate is defined by the annual net operating income (NOI) divided by the cost with the result being a percentage. For example if you buy a home for $100,000 that rents for $1000 per month and has taxes, insurance and management expenses of $400 per month then your NOI is 1000-400 or $600 per month. Following the formula the NOI is $600 X 12 months or $7200. Now divide $7200 by the cost of $100,000 which equals 0.072. That is 7.2% or a CAP rate of 7.2. CAP rates will vary through the market cycle and by location. A high CAP rate yields better return but usually with higher risk, while a low CAP rate equals a lower return and potentially lower risk.

I decided to stay with single-family homes because they give me the best leverage, great cash flow, the best potential appreciation, and are typically the easiest to sell.

Now, I need to talk a little bit about neighborhoods. Real estate jargon typically refers to these as A, B, C and D classes. Class A neighborhoods are the best neighborhoods, nearly all owner-occupied with very few, if any, rentals. At the other end of the spectrum stand the class D neighborhoods. These contain primarily rental homes with just a few properties that are owner-occupied and who have usually been there for many, many years. These neighborhoods tend to be in the most rundown condition and have the highest crime rate. The D neighborhoods often provide excellent cash flow; however, a great deal of energy goes into managing those properties and tenants. Class A neighborhoods typically return a lower cash-on-cash return. Properties in these neighborhoods are often purchased more for their capital appreciation potential. You should know that just because your property is in a class A neighborhood, it does not guarantee you will have a class A tenant.

As you would expect class B and C neighborhoods fall between, with class B having a higher percentage of owner-occupiers than class C neighborhoods. There is no cut and dry line between these two classes of neighborhoods. You can quickly tell when driving through neighborhoods on opposing sides of the spectrum the visual differences between beautifully landscaped A areas to junk cars littering the yards of D areas. Price can also help define neighborhoods. I personally prefer my homes in the C+ to B class neighborhoods. My experience in our local market has shown them to support the best purchase deals, the best cash flow, and the greatest appreciation potential. This is a combination that is hard to bypass.

Each market is different. That's why it is so important that you learn as much as possible about your market before you buy. You may want to concentrate your efforts in one zip code or maybe one school district. Two great sites to help you are www.greatschools.org to see how the local schools rate and www.crimereports.com for just what you imagine, crime stats. When you have learned the housing values within that area you can then expand outward to discern the subtle differences across your community. As you gain this knowledge, you quickly start to centralize your market by cost per square foot. You'll see that crossing a highway, a major boulevard, or a river can bring significant changes to the cost per square foot of very similar homes. In the end the old real estate mantra of location, location, location proves itself to be right over and over again. A home situated on a busy street corner could see a drop in price value of as much as 20% compared to a similar home only a block away. Crossing school district lines can bring huge changes to the value of a home.

There are several ways to jump start your education for your local market. Probably the most common approach is using internet real estate websites such as Zillow.com, Trulia.com and Realtor.com. These websites have all the homes listed in the MLS as well as many for sale by homeowners or FSBOs as they've been nicknamed. These sites also show the asking price of homes that are for sale in all areas of the United States, including yours. Most homes will sell on the retail market from 2% to 8% below their asking prices. Another approach for learning your area quickly is to look through local newspaper real estate ads as well as publications like the Thrifty Nickel and other real estate brochures found in grocery stores. I also like to check Craigslist.com.

The realtor who guided you through the purchase of your present home might be your first power team contact. Ask him or her to let you see a list of all the homes sold in the last thirty, sixty, and ninety day time frames. Tell the realtor you'll be happy with a simple one line listing which will provide the address, square foot, and sold price. This will help you get a quick, current look at what homes are selling for in your various areas. There are also other websites that offer bank-owned properties and foreclosures. HUD, Freddie Mac and Fannie Mae also have websites for homes that banks have returned to them under their insured programs. These homes usually have a time frame of ten to thirty days in which only owner-occupiers can submit offers. After that, investors have the opportunity to submit an offer for these homes.

When you know some basics about your market's housing prices then you need to research what homes will rent for in the areas that interest you. Whenever I am interested in a home, I drive the neighborhood looking for rental signs. I call the phone number listed to find out the size of the house (whether that is provided as square footage or number of bedrooms and baths—preferably both), what they are asking for rent and deposit, the lease time, and if they accept pets. There are also websites that list rentals that you can check as well. In my local market, Catholic Outreach (catholicoutreach.org) provides an Almost Home link free of charge where landlords list properties they have available and renters can see what may match their needs. Finally, nothing beats going door to door and asking renters what they are paying for their home. This last method provides the most factual information.

There are other expenses besides the purchase price you need to be aware of when trying to calculate your overall cost to acquire the property and what the return on your investment may be. Your loan will include an origination fee on the money that you borrow as well as title fees, paperwork and filing fees. These can quickly add up to 2% or more of your purchase price, depending on where you live. You also need to figure in the taxes and insurance for your area. Insurance to cover investment property is less costly than insurance you have on your personal home because you're not insuring any of your personal property. Taxes are taxes. They can vary greatly from ½% to over 3% of your property's value depending on the state/county in which you live.

Don't forget the cost of preparing the home to rent, such as any rehabilitation work that's necessary. Is it in need of a paint job? Is the landscape in decent shape? You'll need to change all exterior door locks and then re-key them every time you bring in a new tenant. What is the condition of the heating and cooling system? What about the hot water heater? Is the roof in good shape? Are there any signs of water damage or mold growth? So, you're going to have to add the cost to have a professional building inspector check the home for you. If you decide to accept any issues spotted by the inspector, you may need to spend money to resolve them before you can rent the home. Are you going to take care of the property yourself or use a property management company? If you do it yourself, remember to calculate in marketing expenses and if you use a property management service the average fee will be around 10% of the rent.

After a couple weeks of taking the steps I listed above, you should begin to have a reasonable idea what the cost of homes are in your market and what they can rent for as well as the local vacancy rate. Now your job is to find the home that you want to invest in. It's very important to remember you're investing in your business, not purchasing the property as your personal home. You do not want to pay retail! I typically try to purchase my homes at a 20% or greater discount to retail. I also figure any repair costs into that discount. For example, if I determine the home has a market value of $150,000 and needs $25,000 work to bring it up to prime condition, I would subtract the $25,000 from the $150,000 price. That leaves a new price of $125,000. I would reduce that by 20% to make an offer of $100,000 or less.

I also calculate a maximum allowable offer based on expectations for rental income and the cost to cover the mortgage, insurance and taxes. Let's use the same $150,000 home in good shape ready to rent. In my market, this home of $150,000 would bring about $1250 in monthly rent. If I paid $150,000 and got an 80% note for thirty years at 5 1/2% interest, I would pay approximately $850 for the P I T I, which stands for principal, interest, taxes and insurance. Figure in 2% for closing costs on this $150K home and this example would require about $33,000 for down payment and closing costs. Since I like to keep things simple, I like return on my money in about five years or less. But with $400 per month gross income (the $1250 rent minus the $850 PITI) divided into $33,000 initial outlay, it would take just shy of seven years to return on my investment if it were fully rented during that time. In this example I have the cash flow but the return is just under 15% and does not meet my minimum return on investment. In this case if I cannot purchase it for less money to reach my return I simply walk away and look for another property.

Chapter 4

Systems Lead to Success

STEP THREE: Set Up Your System - Your Business Guidelines

This chapter will cover the basic system I use for my business. This system works for me. I use it as a basic guideline to find homes whose conditions and prices justify my investment. You may decide to work a different market for your real estate investments. That's fine. But you should still develop your own process that works for you. The use of the system will allow you to expand your business and bring in help. They can follow your proven system, thereby freeing up your time for more productive activities.

To illustrate my system, I will talk about what type of home I look for and why. We will go through the numbers on the first three homes I purchased as an investor. I will do it in detail so you can determine if this is a method you can use to generate cash flow for yourself. While I still hold these first three rentals, I have also invested considerable thought into how I can dispose of or remove these homes from my inventory.

When my wife and I decided to get into real estate investing, we agreed that any property we might acquire could not need more than superficial or cosmetic repairs. For this reason we decided to stay with newer homes on the order of five to fifteen years old. We looked at older homes and multilevel homes, but our best return after considering the work required and doing financial analysis in our market still supported the newer, single-level home. We are both in our early sixties, so we agreed that I did not need to be on two-story roofs to service swamp coolers in the spring and fall. We also stay away from steep pitched roofs. This is pretty easy since we're in a semi-arid climate where very few houses are constructed with a steep pitch.

When we first started looking for a home to invest in, our options were not very restrictive. As we looked at more and more homes, we realized the best model for us would be single-story, newer homes, preferably with vinyl siding, and the standard three bedrooms, two baths, two car garage layout. Homes in this ballpark sell in our community for about $115-$130 per square foot. There are homes in older neighborhoods that fit these criteria and only cost around $80 per square foot. However the older homes tend to need considerably more work before renting for 15% to 30% less than newer homes. Analyses on these older homes show they may bring comparable cash flows but their maintenance requirements are considerably higher and their potentials for capital appreciation are not as strong.

Another consideration for homes is the purchase price and rental income potential. Over the years as my job moved us across five states and the Commonwealth of Puerto Rico, we purchased, built or rented many homes. In markets where the rent was about 6/10 of 1% or less (in this example rent for $600 per month or less per $100K cost) of the value of the home, I determined we were better off renting. However, if the rentals were over 8/10 of 1% then it was usually better to buy, if the economy was in a reasonable cycle. For example, when we lived in Montana, I rented a nice modular home on ten acres valued at about $200,000, but I only paid $450 per month in rent. But in Texas, I built a new home on five acres for $115,000 that would have cost over $1000 per month to rent. In that case my ownership cost was less than the cost of renting. This leads to a

1% rule: you should get at least 1% per month in rent for the purchase price. This will not work in every market, but, if it works in yours, you should have reasonable cash flow.

A lot of people today would be better off buying a home than renting in many markets across the country. But because they have lost their jobs, or been transferred around, they realize it may be better to pay a bit more for rent than tie up a large chunk of money in a down payment on a home that could shackle them to an area they need to leave within two to four years. Some have already lost their homes to foreclosure and their credit has not returned to a level where they can purchase a home, even though they may show more than sufficient income to pay for it.

Whenever we find a house that meets our basic criteria, I do a financial analysis to determine the maximum amount I can pay for the home and get my numbers to work. There are numerous methods to determine your rate of return. Many of these seem unrealistic and do not match up. Let me show you how I calculate my returns. Let's use the easy example of a $100,000 home in which we put 20% down and have 2% closing cost. In this case, my actual cash investment is $22,000 ($20,000 down and $2000 closing cost), assuming I have no repairs needed on the home. The old rule of thumb of 72 can be used to make a quick calculation for your rate of return if you know how long it will take to return your cash investment. If it takes four years to return your money (cash investment) then you divide 72 by 4 and you get an 18% rate of return. Inversely, you can divide 72 by your rate of return; in this case 18%, then you will need approximately 4 years to return your money. For my rate of return of 15%, I divide 72 by 15 to see how long it takes to return my money. I get 4.8 years.

Now let's look at two other methods and see how they compare. Using the same $100,000 home with an investment of $22,000 (again $20,000 down and $2000 closing cost), I need a gross cash flow after PITI of $366 per month to return my investment in five years. To calculate this, I take my $22,000 investment and divide it by 60 months which would require $366 per month to meet my 15% rate of return. A more accurate method would be to take my gross rent and multiply the $366 by 12 to get an annual return of $4392 per year. Since that is my annual return, if we divide it by my initial investment, then $4392 divided by $22,000 returns .199. This represents an annual return of almost 20%. To keep my life simple, my goal is to have a gross rental return of my initial investment on a five-year timeline. I'm willing to be more lax and go out to six years to return my investment if I believe there is a better appreciation potential. At 6 years the 72 rule returns 12% and the more accurate method returns 16.6%.

You must realize there will be repair costs, maintenance costs, and vacancy periods that will extend the timeline to recover my initial investment. By purchasing newer homes, I keep my maintenance and repair costs to a minimum. By providing a better rental value I reduce my vacancy periods. During initial analysis I do not count these, expecting these costs to be offset by the appropriate tax benefits as a buy and hold investor. By doing my own property management, I end up with a much better investment than I received on stocks, bonds and savings during the past ten years. When I consider my capital appreciation potential because I'm buying in a depressed bubble adjusted market and near all-time low interest rates, the risk return far exceeds anything else I might consider.

Let's run through the actual purchases and rents on my first three homes. The first home I purchased from a widow for $122,000 on a conventional loan for 30 years at 5½% interest rate. After taxes and insurance, my PITI on this home is $670. I rented it for $1050 per month (cash flow $380) and increased that rent to $1075 after the first year. I purchased this home in May 2011. It took five weeks to rehab and rent it. The home was built in 1996 on a slab foundation with three bedrooms, two baths and a two car attached garage. It had a new Breezair swamp cooler and a newer hot water heater. It needed flooring throughout and an interior paint job. Our daughter and son-in-law helped me and my wife repaint the house. I lost about two weeks in the rehab process waiting to have new flooring installed. When I include new doorknobs/locks, we ended up with almost $5000 in additional expenses. This gave me a total investment outlay of $31,550 (closing cost, down payment and rehab expenses. etc). Using the rule of 72, it will take me 6.9 years to recover my money at an estimated return of 10.4%. The real return is $380 X 12 = 4550 / 31,550 which yields a 14.4% return.

The market comparison for this home in the summer of 2013 as I write this is approximately $145,000. I have the ability to sell this property myself and net roughly $142,000. If I were to sell it for the $145K and add my cash flow from rent for 2 years and the $12,000 net from my original investment, I would have a return of approximately 33% in 2 years of ownership. With cash flow now over $400 per month and a rising market I am quite happy with this investment.

House number two was a much better deal. It had 1380 square feet built in 2006 and was offered by Fannie Mae. This three bedroom, two bath, three car garage house has central air and heat. I purchased this property for $146,000 at 10% down for thirty years at 5¼%. The total payment for PITI is $874 and it rents for $1250 per month. This house was rent-ready at closing on a Friday and we had a signed one year lease by Sunday (not the typical experience). The rule of 72 shows a return of 18.4%. The actual return is 25½%. Today this house has a marketing comparison value of $190,000. If I did sell it myself, giving 3% to closing costs to the buyers, I end up with a net return of $35,300. Add 22 months' rent to that for a return of $43,600. Divide that by my original investment $17,600 for a total return of 248%. Divide the return by 2 years and the annual rate of return approaches 125%, not a bad investment. As you can see these houses provide solid cash flow return, but if my model was to turn them over every few years the return becomes much better.

We purchased our third house more recently. It is a much smaller home. It has three bedrooms, two baths, and about one half of a garage. This home was a short sale, so I had to pick up the closing costs, but I bought it for $96,400. I received an 80% loan at 4 7/8%, so my PITI was $505. We rented this home in less than a week for $900 with a gross return of $395. Run the same numbers as the previous two, and the Rule of 72 provides a yield of 15.3%. The real rate of return is 22%.

To summarize these first three houses, with the down payments and closing costs and some repairs, we had a total outlay of about $78,000. After the mortgage payments, taxes and insurance, the rents return $1180 per month. That makes the rent role for these three properties just a touch over $14,150. There are always a few expenses, like a garbage disposal or a pilot actuator on a hot water heater, but those are deductible business expenses. So in the end, I have just over $14,000 gross income with $3000 in repair expenses the first year. These three homes net over $11,000 per year in positive cash flow. Because of depreciation, I end up with a loss which can carry over as an offset or reduction toward any ordinary earned taxable income.

This chapter covers the need for systems by detailing my first three purchases. Most businesses are successful because they have systems in place that make every step simple, repeatable and reduce waste. Plan from the very get-go that you will do the same thing with your properties, whether they are single family rental homes, apartment complexes or commercial buildings as you gain experience.

I think the perfect example of systems is McDonald's. Their systems are so refined that part-time, usually high school and college students, run their day to day operations.

Chapter 5

Rev Up the Horsepower in Your Power Team

STEP FOUR: You Need a Power Team

What is a power team? How many people are on it? How do I build it?

It is impossible for you to know everything there is to know about all the different topics that you will be involved with.

Your power team is composed of subject matter experts that fill in the gaps in your knowledge base. Critical members you need to include are a realtor, banker, certified public accountant, an attorney, a mortgage company, bookkeeper, appraiser and trades people, just to name a few.

Another very important member of your power team is a mentor. Unlike most of your power team members or subject matter experts, your mentor is a person who is a proven success in the business you're growing. So if you want to become a buy-and-hold real estate investor, it would help to find someone who is already successful in this branch of real estate investing. This book will provide some guidelines to help you develop a power team composed of subject matter experts and a successful mentor in your local market that can help you immensely.

You must recognize that a mentor will provide a great deal of his/her knowledge and experience as well as their time if they agree to help you. That will come at a cost. Sometimes it will simply be the mentor's way of giving back. Sometimes you may have skill sets that you can trade for his/her services. Other times you may have to go through an educational system to get more detailed training in the area you wish to work in and find a mentor that you can hire to help you along your way.

When I started, I already had a relationship with an excellent realtor. She had helped me buy and sell two homes in my local market. The great thing about her was that she was already a real estate investor. So when I changed my mind set from that of a retail homebuyer to an investor going after great deals, she was very understanding and willing to draw up contracts well below the asking price. As a buy-and-hold real estate investor, she also had many contacts that she was willing to share with me to help develop my power team. For most of you your Realtor will be your first and maybe most important member of your power team.

Another great source to help build your power team is

your local city or county business incubator. We stopped by our business incubator and explained what we wanted to do. They scheduled an appointment for us with two retired professionals— one a banker and one a commercial investor. They provided great input on our business plan as well as a contact list of local accountants, attorneys and small community bankers that might be of assistance.

Let's go back and talk about the real estate agent or broker. I have heard several stories about real estate brokers and mortgage brokers being broker than we are. The point is just being a broker either in the real estate business or in the financial business does not mean they can provide all the services you may need. Because my real estate agent was already an investor she had a vast amount of knowledge that has been very beneficial to me. However, if you do not have that contact, you'll need to interview several real estate agents in several agencies to locate an agent you can work with. I have three basic criteria you should consider. First - they should also be an investor. Second - they need to be highly knowledgeable about your local market. Third - they are a dedicated professional who will work hard for your specific needs.

When you interview some of the realtors, you'll find that some do not want to deal with an investor. They may prefer to work with retail home buyers to make ten or fifteen deals a year and only have to write one contract for each deal. They know that working with an investor will often require as many as ten or twenty contracts to get a single deal negotiated. Even worse, that deal will be 10% to 30% less than the after repair fair market value. This means they have to work hard, they have to write numerous contracts and ultimately receive a lower pay check per unit than they would working with a retail customer. A few may fail to see the benefit of having multiple deals with you and the referrals you may provide through your endeavors. Finally, you must have someone that you can work with, someone that you can build a quick rapport with and you can get along with.

This brings us to another very important point that you need to understand. You are not in competition with realtors or other investors in your real estate business! The more people you come in contact with, the larger the network you build, the more successful your business will become. There will always be contacts you will meet that you cannot personally help. But you may be able to refer them to others within your power team or your network. These referrals will go back to realtors, to investors, to whoever can help them the best. And by them, I mean the person that has a real estate problem. After all, that is all we're doing, helping solve people's problems in real estate. A second important point in this area is that the consistency you use in running your business will have a direct impact on the money you make. Always follow up with everyone you contact! Always follow up with everything you promise!

After you have a realtor who can help you find the type

of home you want to invest in, and there are many methods to find homes without a realtor which we will research later, the next member of your power team needs to be a financial source. There are numerous ways to obtain funds to finance your deals. If you have a good credit score (over 720) and some resources, you can go the traditional route through your mortgage broker or your bank or even a credit union. If your funds are somewhat limited, then you have other options such as joint ventures, limited partnerships and hard money lenders.

I was fortunate to have some resources. I worked with my realtor to find a financial broker used to dealing with investors. To begin my money lender interview process, I put together a package that identified all my resources. It listed my employment income which I documented via two months' worth of verifiable paystubs, then my checking, savings and money market accounts with two months' statements, as well as my IRAs. Financial brokers seemed to be the best in dealing with buy-and-hold thirty-year mortgage rates for investors. The rates and fees were good, and they had all dealt with investors. So I simply picked the person I felt was the most knowledgeable and I got along with the best, and I've been very pleased with him.

Typically, your financial broker will not be able to do short-term interim loans to take care of rehabbing a property as easily as the next contact I will give you. It will be important for you to find a local community bank that deals with businessmen and operates under its own specific guidelines versus that of a large national or international bank conglomerate. This will be the place you want to open your business account and build a relationship with its loan officers. When speaking with the bank, share the same array of papers that you took to your financial broker and update them as your business evolves. You'll likely deal with two different people within this bank: one will be the mortgage banker; the other will be the interim loan business banker. In some banks this will be the same person.

The next members you need to find for your team are a certified public accountant and bookkeeper. I recommend you keep these two people within the same firm if you cannot do your own bookkeeping. If you allow them to do your bookkeeping then they will make sure everything is set to match the tax-preparation software they use. If you do the bookkeeping yourself, you'll need to buy the most current version of QuickBooks software package. I found QuickBooks to be the preferable bookkeeping software for every accountant we interviewed. To complete our selection process, we made appointments with four CPAs on the list provided by our local business incubator and my realtor. We discussed our business plans with each CPA to determine their knowledge levels in real estate investing and their fees. It is also a bonus if your accountant is a real estate investor. These initial interviews are typically free but be sure to ask when you set up the appointment. This turned into a more difficult process for us than I anticipated.

After the interviews, we selected an accountant who then sent a bill for what we thought was a free consultation. Naturally, this ticked me off to no end. Even though we thought he was the most knowledgeable to meet our needs and set the framework for our business, we worried he would nickel and dime us to death throughout our relationship so we bypassed him. We finally selected a national firm that specialized in real estate investors. They proved too expensive for our fledgling business. We have now moved to a third firm. It is local and seems to be just as knowledgeable at half the cost of the national firm.

Your CPA is a critical member of your power team in providing guidance as you develop your business. He or she has a vast amount of knowledge and understanding of our complicated federal and state tax codes. The tax codes consist of a huge tome with thousands of pages. What it essentially says on the first page is if you make money you owe taxes on the money. All the rest of the tax code is nothing more than the IRS detailing ways to reduce your taxes. Every industry has specialized tax codes, exemptions, credits, depreciations and deferrals that allow you to reduce your earned income for that business. If you work at a JOB, you pay income tax, Social Security tax, Medicare tax, hospital tax, taxes for the licenses on your vehicles, taxes on everything you purchase, and sometimes taxes on the taxes. Everyone will take their share before any money goes to you. As a business, you are allowed to claim most of these as deductions if they are legitimate, ordinary and necessary expenses. They reduce your earned income, thereby giving you a lower effective tax rate.

Let me be clear—as I said earlier in the mission statement, you should be running your business as a business. The United States Government and IRS and your state are partners in this endeavor. They set the rules on what to do and what are allowable expenses, and they tell you how to maintain records so they will honor these deductions. If you understand the partnership, it makes you a better business person and provides the documentation that you will need if you're ever audited. The tax codes tell you how to avoid taxes. They do not tell you to evade taxes. This is something you must not do. Once again I should insert that I'm not a qualified tax advisor. I do not intend to represent myself to be professional in matters where you need to consult with your local power team members. Now that's clear, let's return to discussing your power team.

We found this third CPA firm through meetings at our local real estate investors' network. So, you can see, you will want to take advantage of this valuable source of contacts and information. I highly recommend becoming a member of or at least involved with your local real estate investment association. You can ask your realtor for this information or research Meetup.com for groups in your area. You'll meet many like-minded investors who will be more than happy to share names of their power team and even provide advice, guidance and sometimes mentorship as you develop your business. Which brings me to another point about building your power team, you should never be content with your team to the point that you do not consider upgrading when the time arises or be afraid to refresh your standing a bit. One or more of your members may provide too little benefit for their cost during the early stages of your development of your business. It's understandable, even foreseeable, that your business could outpace their ability to provide services you will grow to need.

You are learning there are many people you will develop as part of your power team; your mentor, your financial sources, your CPA, your bookkeeper, and your attorney. All are at the core of the process. But you must also decide if you can hire a property manager or do your own property management. In either case, you need to know a good deal about property management so you will know if you are getting a good manager/management firm or not. To maintain tax advantages as a real estate investment professional, we manage our own properties. That means our team has to be extensive. It incorporates a large number of tradesmen. This includes plumbers and electricians, HVAC service personnel, painters, floor installers, roofers, irrigation workers, even jack-of-all-trades handymen to name a few.

We are lucky that one of our close friends is both a master electrician and general contractor and has lived in the community his entire life. He helps me when I can't get others in a timely fashion to do the job to the specifications I require. He also recommends other trades people that I use as needed. As your business grows large enough or you acquire beyond the single-family unit to apartment units, you'll likely find yourself in a position where you need to hire a part-time or even a full-time handyman to do all the small tasks like fixing a leaky commode or faucet. And, don't forget those seasonal maintenance issues. In our semi-arid region those include winterizing swamp coolers and blowing out irrigation lines in preparation for winter. Each region has its own requirements. Be sure you have someone reliable to follow through on those for you.

The above example with my friend shows how important it is to build relationships. These relationships will help you make contacts with people you need in order to build your business. They also make life more enjoyable because when you build good relationships, opportunities eventually arise to send business to your friends and helping others is always a great feeling.

Anecdote: When we purchased our second rental home, we used the same home inspector recommended to us during our first rental home purchase. This second time around he gave us a 10% discount for the repeat business. We met him at the house for a review of what he'd done and seen. We discussed the fact that I spent more on the flooring in our previous house than I had anticipated. He immediately wrote down the contact info for the man who held the national contract with many government entities to install carpet in foreclosed homes. I called and discussed his pricing. I quickly found out I could have saved over 25% if I had had that contact when we installed flooring in our first house. You can bet he's in my contact list for the next time I have floors that need replacing.

One last point for this chapter: You're the leader. Your team is for guidance and advice. You make the final decisions. Do not take "No" for an answer if part of your team says you can't do something you propose. Follow up! Ask them HOW can we do this? If they cannot help you find a way, it may be time to replace someone on the team.

Chapter 6

Show Me the Money

STEP FIVE: Funding

Funding is vital to move your business forward. Many people watch real estate investment late-night TV shows. They buy books and go to training. They follow the business plan laid out for them and start making calls. They go see the houses. But...they are afraid to take the next step because they simply do not know how to acquire the finances necessary to close the deal.

If you have funds and good credit yourself as I explained in an earlier section, it's not that difficult to obtain financing to buy your investment homes. But, there is a limit. When we first started buying houses, we could only have four mortgages. That was part of the new banking regulations due to an overreaction to the housing meltdown. Mortgage limits recently increased to ten. You need to understand that even with the more flexible number of mortgages you can hold, you still have to meet debt to income ratios and have enough money available through your savings and investments accounts to satisfy the underwriters if you use traditional financing.

Having your own funds available allows you to use the traditional method like I did and leverage your financing through mortgage brokers. In my case, I placed 10% to 20% down on my homes. Another approach is to purchase a house outright, clean it up, and put a tenant in it. Then, go to your local community bank or mortgage broker and show them that you own the home and want to finance it. You can typically get 70% of your investment back to do other deals. You may have to mature the rent roll a full year at which time you could get a 70% loan based on a new appraisal. Either way leaves you 30% invested in the house. Often, by properly rehabbing the house to good condition and placing a tenant in it, you might obtain slightly better terms. If you buy the house right, say 20% to 30% below market value, and mature it for a year with tenants in place, you may end up with more cash after you finance it than you invested in the property. Repeat this process as many times as you can and you are on your way to a great portfolio of rental homes.

Whether you have your own money or do not have your own money, using other people's money is preferable whenever you can do that. OPM, or other people's money, is a great way to start your real estate investment business. The great thing about OPM is if you have a great deal; dollars will follow that deal. If you don't have a great deal; then it is unlikely you will obtain financing using OPM. Hard money lenders can be the answer for really great deals. They typically charge 2% to 5% origination fees and 10% to 15% interest annually. Often they will have a minimum fee, but for a great deal you want to control this can be a good option.

No matter whose money you use, you must stick to your requirements that you set up in your business plan for cash flow and return on investment. If you want to successfully make money in the real estate business, I believe the best way is to buy right for cash flow. If you buy right, the property already has capital appreciation (equity) built into the purchase. That should provide your buffer and reduce the risk from any additional decline in the housing market. So if you purchased the property at the right price and have substantial or at least reasonable cash flow, you can ride out declines both in market depreciation and/or reduced rents over time.

When you have funded several deals, either with your own money or others', you improve your skills and ability to make workable tweaks to your business plan and you can expand into other purchases through the partner process. This might be set up as a limited liability partnership or a joint venture. In these scenarios, you bring your knowledge of real estate investing and property management to others who simply do not have the time or desire to learn enough about the business to find the great deals available to them. They can, however, provide their credit to acquire additional financing or mortgages if you have run up against the mortgage limit wall or your debt ratio has stopped your progress.

Who might be available to add their money to your knowledge and efforts to purchase great deals? The first option for many will be family and/or friends. Many times professions, like doctors and attorneys, are looking for property investment deals but do not have the time to find those deals. Start thinking about and asking anyone you know that might have money to invest. If nothing else you may pick up tidbits of advice or a reference that could make your next deal a real paycheck.

When you own multiple homes, you may decide to group them into a single commercial loan. This is referred to as a portfolio loan and can be obtained through your local community bank. The great thing about a commercial loan is it's calculated on the CAP rate or the return on investment potential that the properties provide. Another important factor is the relationship you have developed with the bank. Once those mortgages are moved into a commercial loan, they no longer count against your personal mortgage limits. So if you hold ten mortgages and/or have reached a limit on mortgages, then consider moving four or five into a single commercial loan. That would open an opportunity for more mortgages. As your relationships grow in the financial community and you prove over a few years that your business makes money, the banks may proactively come to you to lend you more money.

This next section is dedicated to those who have no money, poor credit, and yet harbor a desire to move into real estate investment. The number one option for you may be wholesaling. What is wholesaling? Think of it this way: find a great deal, put it under contract and then assign that contract to a real estate investor who has the cash funds to close the deal. For example, you look for distressed properties, or distressed owners, in a number of ways. You make offers. You lock a property under contract for half or less of the market value of the home. If you plan to go the wholesaling route you should build a buyers list of real estate investors or home rehab contractors who express interest in taking over your signed contract.

Homes that are in poor condition and disrepair are often passed over by retail buyers. These properties need too much work for the typical retail buyer. In these cases, the properties are distressed. Very often the homeowners are also distressed.

Through job changes, family upheavals or their need to move elsewhere within a shrinking timeframe, they are at their wits ends as to how to sell their properties. This is where you can create a win/win/win situation. You assess how much work needs to be done and then tell them you and your investor buy properties wholesale, but in order to make a profit in this circumstance; you can only offer X dollars for their home. How do you arrive at the price you give as a maximum allowable offer (MAO)? We'll use the following example: You look at a house in a particular neighborhood that you believe should bring $100,000 after it's repaired and cleaned up. This is the ARV or After Repair Value. You estimate it needs $20,000 in repairs—maybe a new roof, new carpet, HVAC system, interior/exterior paint, etc. Now, think about the end investor, the person to whom you'll sell the house. If it's a rehab contractor they will want a buffer profit of about $30,000 on the deal. With $20K needed for repairs and $30K for the rehab profit that means that on a

$100,000 house, you can offer no more than $50,000. Now add in a $5000 wholesale fee for yourself and the maximum allowable offer (MAO) is $45,000 on that house. There are numerous books on wholesaling and if this is the route you have to follow please acquire and consume several of them.

This is where attending real estate associations or networking meetings and having built a network comes in handy. When you find the right deal you call rehab people on the contact list you created through your networking. Tell them you have a house that they can make a $30,000 profit on after repairs. Give them the address so they can go see the property. If they are interested, tell them that for $5000 you will assign the contract to them. They pay you $5000, you sign over the $45,000 contract and walk away from the deal. Depending on the market you are in, you may be able to find three to twenty or more of these deals a year. This can help raise you out of debt and earn money which you can then invest into longer-term holding investments.

Another way to obtain properties without much, if any, cash is the lease option method. Lease option is a lease under which the leasee has the right to purchase the property. Various kinds are available, such as lease options to buy a personal residence, purchase lease options, sandwich lease options, fixer-upper lease options, and multi-unit lease options. There're also options with a lease primarily used for purchasing undeveloped land.

Since lease options include such a large category of real estate business, I will not get into too much of them now but will provide a single simple example. This is a textbook example of someone that has to move to another area because their job transfers them. This is another circumstance when you have to run the numbers closely to make sure it works for you. It may be that you submit a lease option to buy, say during the next twenty-four months, and explain to the present owner that you will work with the bank to transfer the note responsibility to you. You will also put one of your approved tenants into the property with an agreement they will buy it as soon as they clean up their credit report. Rather than walk away with a short sale or foreclosure that affects their credit for years, this provides the owner an opportunity to get out from under the property for a few thousand dollars while you take over responsibility to pay the note. Using this process, you may get into properties for no money down. You may even have money put into your pocket from the current owner. This can happen when you manage their property by putting renters in place with the option to buy within some future period of time that is mutually agreeable. The new tenants have an opportunity to clean up their credit and you pocket a bit of cash flow until the tenant buys the property from you. This method is referred to as a sandwich lease option.

Another method is to search for deals where the owner carries the financing. You will typically pay closer to market price for these homes, because the owner takes a lower down payment.

This is a good method in an appreciating market. Remember this book is about cash flow and very few beginning investors will understand the market well enough to manage this speculative approach.

Wholesale and lease option strategies can work for anyone who is driven to improve cash flow and is willing to hustle to make the steps happen. These strategies are primarily for those with little-to-no cash and less-than-perfect credit. As you can see from this chapter, there are several ways you can generate income in real estate. Real estate has built-in advantages to help you quickly create wealth. The key to making money in real estate is to be open to various methods or approaches to generate deals. Once you see the deals then you have to determine the ones that meet your criteria and work for the market you invest in. In the end the formula I am sharing is to **buy right and have cash flow.**

Chapter 7

Marketing - The Key to Success

STEP SIX: Marketing

From the very beginning of your business incubation you should think about how you market your business. This means a great deal more than just advertising properties. Branding is the key to successful marketing. If you see a red aluminum can or a Mae West figure bottle you immediately know it's Coke. Coke has done a tremendous job successfully branding their company. Branding involves visual imagery, catchy phrases, jingles and many other clever ideas that quickly connect the synapses in your brain from memories to the product itself. If I use the phrase snap-crackle-pop, what immediately comes to your mind? That's right, Rice Krispies. And how many of you heard that snap-crackle-pop when you poured milk over Rice Krispies? Nobody! But this catchy phrase is ingrained through years of watching Kellogg's commercials although a snap-crackle-pop sound is not what we hear.

This is something you want to think about for your real estate business as well. How will you put your brand out for the public to see? Primarily you will do it through the Internet because it is your least expensive vehicle and most cost beneficial tool available today. You can develop websites. You may specialize in websites for buyers or websites for renters, even websites for sellers. Each one of those may have a different catchy phrase. You may segregate them into three different DBAs, that is "doing business as" in your primary LLC. Here is an important note - do not let the lack of a website or knowing your brand be an excuse against getting started. You can always change the name of your company, your DBA, and even the structure of your business entities.

Social networking is now a big deal in business. To be successful, you need a power team member that can handle websites and keep all your information updated and timely on your web links, Facebook, Twitter and LinkedIn just to name a few. To keep people coming back, you need to provide fresh content on your sites so they want to see how your new information may apply to them. A good approach is to brainstorm a dozen easy-to-write content items. They should provide quick information in a simple to read format that encourages your e-visitor to opt-in to your website through a squeeze page for more information.

What is a squeeze page? You see them every time you visit a website and link to something that interests you. When that little pop-up box appears and asks for your name, your address, your email, your phone number, in order to get additional information; those are squeeze pages or jump pages. Marketing software captures the information provided and automatically feeds it into a database so additional useful content directed to that person's interest can be sent. Your potential customer receives the information you offered and you get a new, hopefully motivated contact.

As an example, let's assume you already have a seller's website. A dozen topics pop into mind that would interest your visitors. You have seen these on websites you visit—clickable headlines like Five Steps Through the Foreclosure Process; What is a Short Sale; How to get a Loan Modification to Reduce Your Payment; and How to Improve Your Credit Score. If you have a good integrated client-based software, it can segregate everybody that comes in through these individual squeeze pages to a specific

contact list under the appropriate category. Really good software

provides additional contact methods such as automatic email,

postcard or letter printouts that can be calendared for follow-up

with the new prospects.

Let's say your website is *John's Houses For Sale*, with a

catchy slogan such as "Let John Get you the Most House for

Less Money." Your website also has links to secondary pages on

buying a home, living under the threat of foreclosure, selling your

home as a short sale, how to improve your credit, etc. Each week

you rotate the contents listed on the front page. Jane comes in to

see what to do now that she has gotten a foreclosure notice from

the bank. Your secondary page on foreclosure has several

clickable opportunities that take Jane to a squeeze page where she

enters her information. Your software immediately sends a

response to Jane with a thank you for her inquiry stating your

pleasure to be able to help and providing the information she requested. You may also set your software to remind you to send another email or postcard or phone call to Jane in three days with another one in a week and another in two weeks. Your software settings keep you on track to do the proper follow-up. Remember what I said earlier - he who is most consistent makes the most money.

When you set up your website, it is beneficial to target a specific audience with a separate URL. You do not want to confuse or irritate a seller coming into your site with content information you have for hard money lenders and investors, or an article on how to make profit from helping sellers in this down market. Each of these content areas has an appropriate place. You want your URL to target the specific customer that you will be serving.

Marketing is an entire book all by itself so I have kept this section fairly brief. We use REIBlackBook to automate our marketing. You will find additional content in the bonus section available on my website:

www.cashflow7stepstosuccessfulrealestateinvesting.com

Chapter 8

The Joy of Tenants

STEP SEVEN: Property Management

Property management can quickly make or break your business especially if you're in the buy-and-hold area of real estate. You have two methods of approach to property management; one is do-it-yourself and the other is to hire it done. We do it ourselves. I will go into some detail, a lot of which we learned during the past few years. Even if you plan to hire professional property management you should pay attention to this chapter. Understanding the basics of property management will allow you to clarify expectations and have a better relationship with a professional property manager.

Let's say your mortgage broker arranged a preapproved loan for you, and you found a house that met your needs. You offered a contract to buy the home right. The seller accepted. If you have not already done so, you need to take certain steps to get ready to rent this property. If you have not set up your own lease, you need to do that now and have it reviewed by your attorney. During the contract process, you have several other things to do like have the house inspected to verify there are no surprises. Make sure all you're funding is in place and you're able to hand over a cashier's check at closing. Review all closing costs with your financial broker. You may need to have the house or property surveyed, and you have to get an appraisal. An appraisal for your rental home will cost more than the appraisal you did when you purchased your home. This is because it is a two prong appraisal. First is to ascertain the value of the home and second is to do a rental survey to help the financial broker determine at what dollar level the house will most likely rent. Continue to work in coordination with your financial broker, your realtor, and the title company if necessary to make sure things remain on track. It's imperative to meet all timelines on the contract which will allow you to back out if you find an unexpected surprise.

You also need to be thinking about how to rent the property. Hopefully you've done your own rent surveys; you've gotten suggestions from your realtor and have the results of the rental appraisal to help you determine an asking price. You also should know what work has to be done to the property after closing and before your new tenant can move into it. Be prepared to get that work done in a timely manner. Our first property needed new carpet and vinyl plus paint throughout. You might count this as your basic cleanup. Since I was still working full time then, I figured that using our weekends and evenings, we could get this done in two weeks. It took three because the carpet company failed to get an installation contractor to the property as scheduled.

During the contract period you also need to consider your marketing approach—how much you will rent for, what the deposit will be and the terms of your lease. Will you offer a six month lease or require a one year lease? Will you allow pets? All these options need to be considered for your marketing approach. There are well over thirty sites on the Internet that people can use to find homes for rent. These include rent.com, hotpad.com, craigslist.com, trulia.com just to name a few. You can go to each of these sites individually and post your information. However, in my case, I have really cool software that allows me to post information about the property in one place and then it posts to over forty websites. It also creates a

PDF flyer I print and post in nearby laundromats, supermarkets, restaurants, and it formats my ad into HTML that I can easily post on craigslist.com. Awesome, right!! We have been so successful with our approach that we provide excess names and phone numbers to other landlords at our real estate investment network meetings simply because we want to help them and we have nothing available to rent.

I must restate here if you're a buy-and-hold real estate investor it is a business and not a hobby and managing your properties is a business and not a hobby. Do not let your tenants train you to their needs. Sometimes it will be very tough but you must follow the rules and guidelines you lay out every time, all the time so if you end up in front of a judge you can stand by the words of your lease. The lease is a very important contract between you and your tenants. It defines rules and regulations that you expect each of you (landlord and tenant) to live by, including special guidelines such as covenants and requirements within a homeowners association that governs restrictions on other residents and pets. Your lease is the golden grail between you and your tenants. I included a sample lease for you to see at my website: www.cashflow7stepstosuccessfulrealestateinvesting.com. It is a combination derived from Colorado leases found online and two provided by friends in the rental business.

Do not use this lease for the area you live in without your attorney's approval. I repeat again do not use this lease until it has been checked for legalities within the state and county that you will use it. I make no claims that this lease will hold up under any court of law for anyone else.

If you intend to manage your own properties, you need to visit your county clerk's office or judicial office and learn the eviction process. Sometimes it's very simple and easy to accomplish, and a tenant can be evicted within ten to twenty days from the posting of notice. In states where tenant's rights far outweigh landlord's rights, it can be very difficult, even taking several months to obtain relief and evict a bad tenant. Fortunately where I live and in the states where I hope to conduct business in the future, the process is fairly well-defined. It can be applied in an easy step-by-step manner and completed in a reasonable timeframe. In some jurisdictions the number of rental properties that you own could determine the process you have to go through and the timeframe it will take to evict your tenant.

Real estate investment clubs provide the opportunity to meet many local landlords. They can be beneficial in helping you find power team members and can also offer information garnered from their experiences and intended to help you understand local rules and guidelines. The information is often tempting to use, but you must verify anything you hear with your power team. In the past two years I bet I've heard thirty times I can do this or cannot do that only to find out the guidance was inaccurate or completely wrong after discussing it with my legal and accounting team members.

But, to get back to the lease: In addition to it, you also need an application for the tenants to fill out and a checklist on the property condition for them to complete and return to you. The application is a critical part of screening your tenants to determine if you believe they can live in your house or not. Failure to follow-up on application information will result in your living through any number of the hundreds if not thousands of horror stories about rentals instead of the tens of thousands of success stories that are never heard about landlords with wonderful tenants. I screen tenants to verify their job and their current and past rental history. I require paystub copies or other verifiable forms that show their gross pay equals a minimum of three times the monthly rent for my property. I have homes I will allow pets in and homes I will not. Household pets are not a protected group, therefore I have the right to determine as I see fit. If I check one of my properties where I do not allow pets, and find an animal there, even if the tenant says they are only babysitting it, I start the eviction process. For those homes where I allow pets, I collect a premium deposit and/or charge extra money on the rent. This is not posted as part of the rental price. I simply indicate I may accept pets but additional deposits and rents will apply. As an example you may not wish to take cats because their urine is almost impossible to deodorize. You might consider small or maybe medium dogs so you may put a limit of forty pounds. You certainly wouldn't consider vicious breeds; however, many purebreds and mixed breeds make excellent pets and widen your tenant pool.

Part of our mission statement and goals were to have the best house at the best price available in the area. If you try to rent your home in a good rental market and it is not leased within ten days, you probably missed the target price. Sometimes it's as simple as a psychological number. You may find after you close on the house that your mortgage principal, taxes, HOA fees and insurance total $825 per month. You want to make $400 gross rent on this house and know that the rental market is $1175 to $1250. So you can market it at $1225/month to reach the $400 per month cash flow or it may be better to advertise it for $1195 and have more tenants to screen which results in better renters in a shorter vacancy time frame. Then you can go up on your rent an average of 2% or more each year, or whatever your lease timeline is, to increase your margin.

One way to keep costs low and your product consistent is to pick paint colors for inside and out as well as carpet, tile, vinyl colors and styles. Make decisions on all the little maintenance items that come up day-to-day or hopefully just year-to-year like light bulbs, batteries for detectors, switch plates, mini-blinds, etc. Make them all alike and then it's possible to buy in bulk.

Decide what paint brand you will use. I like Sherwin Williams. Their colors are consistent and repeatable over other base paints, and I get the uniform look I want. So make a plan to always use an off shade of white such as a shell, antique or something like that. Whatever you choose, stay with the same color all the time. That way you never have any waste. If you have two gallons left in a five gallon bucket you can use it at another property that needs refreshing rather than storing it until the tenant moves. I prefer white mini-blinds for window treatments. They provide the required privacy, light and shading all in one with no holes in the walls. You can use whatever vendor you want to give you the best value in your area such as a Lowe's, Home Depot, or even Walmart.

If your homes rent at some cutoff value in your market, you can use vinyl floor in the laundry, kitchen, baths and dining room and carpet throughout the rest of the house. While I only replaced the flooring in one home so far, I now have an agreement with a local corporate vendor to buy rental quality stock carpet in the same color and weight produced from their mill year in and year out. That way, I can use it without the need to redo the whole house. If the house breaks above a certain rent point, vinyl will not be sufficient. You will need tile flooring. You may find in some cases that you can lay the tile floor down almost as cheap as vinyl. This would provide an upscale look for a home that was intended for slightly lower rental market.

Sidebar antidote: A young man who just graduated with a chemical engineering degree was in town looking for a house. He and his roommate worked as interns with a local energy company. He liked everything about our house until we reviewed the application and lease agreement. He did not want to write his social security number on the application. I told him he did not have to provide this information, but if he didn't we would consider it incomplete and disregard his application. Sometimes you have to educate young people entering the real world for the first time so they recognize that landlords can insist Social Security and driver's license numbers are included on applications and leases or they will wind up living in their cars. At the other end of the extreme, we had a very nice couple show up to look at our house. They brought their bank statements, pay stubs, tax returns and car loan agreements to show they had sufficient funding and income to rent our home.

People may make fun of you for wanting to become a landlord. They may refer to you as a slumlord. It's important you do not agree with either assessment. You're an owner. You provide safe, affordable, clean housing for people who, for whatever circumstances, cannot or will not buy their own home at the current time. Some people report property management is a thankless, never-ending job of dealing with tenants, toilets and termites as if they were all in the same category. Believe me, they are not. We meet wonderful people during the interview and application process for our homes. With our marketing, we receive numerous calls and have shown an open property to over half a dozen people the same day. We continue to show the property until an applicant passes the application process and provides verifiable funds for the deposit and first month's rent.

This brings us back to the joy of tenants. The first of the month rolls around and I go to the mailbox and start picking up checks. It is always great to get a check that's a third higher than my mortgage. However, in our first three homes, we do have a couple that have trouble managing their money and tend to be consistently late. By late, I mean the third through the sixth day of the month...on one occasion the tenth. Recently, we had a check returned for insufficient funds. Be sure to send monthly statements to people like this. Let them know how much they incurred in late fees and that you assess a 1.5% per month interest on those late fees until they pay in full. Once I receive the tenant's second late payment or returned check, I immediately send a letter to the tenant letting them know the rent is due on the first and that the grace period to the fifth of the month is a privilege not a right. I inform them that thereafter I will charge late fees beginning on the second day of the month. Or, they will get a letter stating that I will no longer take their personal checks. From that point onward, they must pay rent via verifiable funds, either in the way of money order or cashier's check mailed to my company address. I also explain that cash will not be accepted since I do not want them tracking me down, and I will not make special trips to meet them, write a receipt, and then have to go to the bank and possibly make an after-hours deposit.

So the cool part about tenants is they mail their payments to you, that payment covers the mortgage and provides extra money for positive cash flow. You can use it to expand your real estate business or supplement your living expenses. And, contrary to all the horror stories you hear, most tenants appreciate the fair value you provide. It's in a safe neighborhood close to amenities they want, so they respect and care for your property, showing pride in where they live.

Chapter 9

Go Build Your Wealth!

WRAP UP: Execution

This chapter is all about action! Why did you read this book? Are you satisfied with the status quo of your life? Are you making all the money you can ever spend and building all the wealth that you want for yourself and your family? Maybe you're just barely getting by but want a better life for yourself and your family, or maybe you have a great job making more than adequate income but are fed up with your 401(k) turning into a 101K. It's a fact nobody and I mean nobody will take care of your money better than you.

Some of you are moving forward and simply want to expand your knowledge with a different view of how I invest. I congratulate you for taking action. Sharing my experience is what drove me to write this book. Maybe you can serve as a mentor for someone looking to get started. For those that have not taken action, maybe the rest of this chapter can help you.

Maybe you don't think you can do this. Maybe you don't think you have the education, knowledge, time or the motivation to change your life. Let me quote Henry Ford: "Whether you think you can, or you think you can't, you're right." I cannot make you get out of your easy chair and out from in front of the TV to take action to make a new life for yourself. You need to look inside yourself and truly ask, truly answer two questions. Am

I satisfied with where I am? Will I be in the same situation one year from now, five years from now or at the end of my career?

I remember when I was a kid we used to jokingly pass around the phrase "…if you could go around the world for a nickel, I could not back out of the driveway…." Is that a self-fulfilling mindset to be poor? I think it was! Go to Netflix and order the DVD, "The Secret". This is a start to understanding you deserve to have all your desires. To be the best you can be. There is nothing wrong with being rich. Think of all the good you can do for your church, community and your family.

Do you attend every introductory seminar that comes to a town near you offering a path to a new life but never follow through? Maybe the training is too expensive, but there are other avenues you can take. Local libraries have many of the guru books. Check out website access like www.biggerpockets.com and sign up for their free account. Please be sure to attend local real estate meetings to interact with other investors.

Do you read books about how to start a business? Is this your second, twelfth or twentieth book about how to invest in real estate? Are your shelves or e-reader stuffed with books on how to improve yourself, how to lose weight, how to become a better person? Do you read any of those books or do you just buy them and then watch them collect dust? Do you read them, but never try to change using their guidance?

Do you dream about a different life, one with time for fun or travel with your family? Do you wish you could provide better education for your kids, your grandkids? Do you contribute to your church, but not as much as you wish you could? Do you think about volunteering if only you had more time? Do you consider helping those who have less than you but do nothing?

I could probably put together a ten volume edition of great motivational quotes from all the successful people we know in public life. There are many more from people not known to all. But in the end, the choice is yours. You can continue down the same path you have always followed, or you can choose a different fork on the road you travel. You can **choose** to take a risk. You can hear your family and friends say you can't do that. And, you can **choose** to ignore their opinions.

The book *Rich Dad Poor Dad* was the catalyst for me. It does not read like a great literary work, but it got the point across. It opened my mind to a different point of view, a different way to evaluate risk and most importantly a different way to think about money. If you're ready to make the change, let's review the seven steps I outlined.

Step One: Develop a business plan.

Define your mission, describe your business purpose, set up your business goals, create your entity structure and get your tax ID number.

Step Two: Learn your market.

Location! Location! Location! Buy Right! Buy Right! Buy Right! What a simple formula. Execution is the key.

Step Three: Set up your system.

Know your system. Set your plan and work the plan. Never buy if the numbers do not work.

Step Four: Power Team.

This doesn't have to occur at once but it will gradually build until you have a number of competent subject manner experts you count on for good advice and quality work.

Step Five: Funding.

Your approach here is largely determined by what kind of resources you have or do not have. Be honest and work the methods that best fit your available resources.

Step Six: Marketing.

Marketing is critical. The real goal in marketing is to build a quality list of both buyers and sellers, and to advertise your product to your target audience.

Step Seven: Property Management.

Approach this in a professional way and your real estate business will take off.

Those are your seven steps to successful cash flow in real estate investing. Now it's up to you! Are you going to fall through? Or, are you going to follow through?

Remember this, for all the people that go through real estate investment courses from Rich Dad Education, Dean Graziosi, Ron LeGrand, or any other real estate guru, the results still come down to what **YOU** do. You must take action. We can debate all day the ins and outs of these real estate educators, but they all have systems that work for them and many of their students. However, for every successful testimonial you hear from them, there are hundreds that spent good money to enroll in their classes and still did nothing. The key for each of you to turn your dream into reality will be discipline.

For my wife and me, our goal is to buy real estate right and manage it to build wealth so we can educate our kids and grandkids in financial literacy. I am a great fan of Robert Kiyosaki's *Rich Dad Poor Dad* and agree wholeheartedly that the education system in America has totally failed all of our citizens when it comes to financial literacy. To prove this statement all you have to do is look to the five hundred thirty five so-called best and brightest public servants in America that go to the Beltway with honorable intentions but who have run this country into debt to the tune of over $17 trillion. (See www.usdebtclock.org) In the end this will be a headwind for all of us via increased taxes, higher inflation from all the fiat money being printed not only in America but globally. It will create an even bigger gap between the haves and have-nots and the continued demise of America's middle class. My final word; use the many bonus websites I included and visit my website for this book to see additional bonus material and updated information at: www.cashflow7stepstosuccessfulrealestateinvesting.com

Thanks for staying with me. I wish you the very best and Happy Investing for cash flow.

Made in United States
Orlando, FL
05 July 2025

62661812R00061